Liking in Silence

Liking in Silence

Poems by Kim Sa-in

Translated by
Brother Anthony of Taizé and Susan Hwang

WHITE PINE PRESS / BUFFALO, NEW YORK

White Pine Press
P.O. Box 236
Buffalo, NY 14201
www.whitepine.org

Poems from *Liking in Silence,* Changbi Publishers, Inc., 2006, and poems from *Beside a Baby Donkey,* Changbi Publishers, Inc., 2015, are published by arrangement with Changbi Publishers, Inc., Seoul, South Korea.

The following poems were published in Volume Four of the review *Azalea* (Korea Insititute, Harvard University, 2011): "Cosmos Flower," "Someone Who Makes a Bridge Feel Lonely," "Springtime Sea," "A Flower," "Rice Cake."

The following poems were published in *The Iowa Review,* Volume 43, Number 3 (Winter 2013/14) "Rainy Season," "Springtime Sea," "A Flower."

This book was translated and published with the support of the Daesan Foundation.

Printed and bound in the United States of America.

ISBN 978-1-945680-34-2

Library of Congress number 2018968435

Contents

from *Beside a Baby Donkey* (2015)

Why I Write The Way I Write

Kim Sa-in

This text was originally written in 2010 for presentation at the start of Kim Sa-in's participation in the University of Iowa's International Writing Program.

I. Solidarity of Sorrow

A few days ago, I saw an American movie entitled, *Winter's Bone.* It was about the wretched lives of people expelled to a desolate mountain region. My heart ached as I watched that dark, sad film. At the same time, the film ironically comforted me with the realization that "Ah, this country, America, has the same misery and despair that we have in South Korea. We're not that different, after all." This realization came back to me with the Iranian movie, *Turtles Can Fly,* and the Indonesian movie, *The Rainbow Troops.* The scenes of war, poverty, and misery in the three films drew me closer to America, Iran, and Indonesia, because these scenes were not so different from what I had experienced in my country.

The sense of shared pain, sorrow, and shame brings people closer to one another. It makes people intimate. We're comforted when we meet people who have the same scars. It makes us laugh and tell jokes, even through the pain. As you know, misery consists of something other than bitterness: often we find unexpected humor and excitement in it. During my residency at the International Writing Program, I want to discover the scars, agonies, and darkness of America more than anything else. In doing so, I want to confirm that we are one as humans and to come closer to America. That's the power of pain: powerful solidarity based on shared sorrow.

I was born in 1956 in a poor rural village in South Korea and grew up through the era of developmentalism and authoritarianism. Today, the Olympic games, the World Cup tournament, Samsung cell phones, LG television, and Hyundai cars are symbols of South Korea, a newly-emerging economy. However, they're only one face of the country. The other side of Korean society still struggles with indelible scars from the past four decades, such as the division of North and South Korea and the fierce ideological contestation originating from this division, a military dictatorship that lasted until the end of the 1980s, and rapid industrialization and urbanization driven by authoritarian regimes. What we gained in return for deserting our cherished values, or for selling our souls, was money; specifically, money in the hands of a few. You already know that unjustly earned money is as fatal as poverty to humanity. I'm sure other developing countries would share such experiences.

When I started writing in this social atmosphere, to be faced with the question of how my writing can empower suffering neighbors was inevitable. South Korean writers of my generation, including myself, were ashamed of writing in a way that only elite readers could appreciate or that exaggerated the writer's own suffering. My writing became more bitter and louder with hatred of unjust power and the brazenness of the "haves." Simultaneously, I got involved in the social movement to express my hatred and rage. Since the late 1970s, I've been imprisoned three times and have had to hide with pseudonyms from the oppressive regimes. It was not until ten years ago that I first obtained my passport.

In 1987, the democratization movement and the sacrifices of many people brought formal democracy to Korea. As the primary goal was attained, I lost direction for my literary energy. Reflecting on myself, I realized that my poetry was contaminated by an excessive sense of duty, dogmatism, and frightening hatred. That realization was something like the shock of seeing the face of the enemy in the mirror. I saw the face of a miserable utilitarian who takes advantage of people in the name of people.

In the early 1990s when I returned to my normal life, I had to struggle to overcome dogma and hatred. When I lose the ability to appreciate things as themselves, when I lose compassion and sympathy, I cannot call myself a poet. When I lose humility toward the world and life in the circuit of my mind, I fail to reach the true name of anything, even grass or a stone. Since this time in my life, my writing has been marked by the same struggle to recover this humility and appreciation.

The self-reflective practice should be continued, and my entire life might not be enough. However, only when humble self-emptying is attained, or at least when I struggle to attain it, I'm a poet and not a poetry specialist. I dare say that I have practiced God's work since God in Genesis called each being's true name. This is not news; poets of all ages and all countries have pursued this role. However, this is my only weapon against the terrible power of commercialization and the spell of money. Please forgive me if my way is too conservative and archaic. Still I believe this is a place where someone should stay behind and preserve.

I would like to conclude by talking about my "prayer" of late, which expresses my resolution to write poetry.

II. Poetry as a Devotion

For me, one of the most precious words in Korean is *Seomgim,* which means giving service, or devotion. Just getting my tongue around this word makes me feel a little more docile and pure. Though I'm afraid it might be presumptuous, I humbly pray that in my activity as a poet, I may serve even in some small way all the unconsidered things in the world. My hope is that the warm, pure passivity denoted by *Seomgim* will enable my writing to arrive at a certain earnestness in both its content and form.

Rather than busily assert their own opinions, I want my poems to be heard by others. I look for poetry that waits in silence rather than rushes forward, one that, rather than readily reveals its own ideas, can be patient when patience is needed.

I want it to be a poetry of the defeated rather than of the victors. Even though bright, loud laughter is fine and seductive, I believe that the complete spiritual world can always be revealed in sorrow and bitterness. However, I would not be so bold as to claim that my poetry is written on behalf of the weak and overlooked.

I see writing poetry as something like standing together in the rain, beside the grass and the exposed trees. I would never insist that the best solution for dealing with the rain is to bring someone an umbrella. Standing side by side with those exposed to the cold rain of loneliness and sad resignation, I pray that I can console them, and thereby offer them a part of my umbrella, and also a part of my righteous anger. To be a victim with pleasure, to lose faithfully, that is my chosen path to victory. I'm willing to take this as my metaphor and my metonymy as my principle of realism and subversion. Furthermore, if possible, I really hope to take this also as the principle underlying my ecological imagination and my feminism.

Finally, if these wishes are too ambitious, I earnestly desire that my poetry will at least avoid hurting others. I will never try to exploit the names of grass and stones, to embellish my poetry, nor its true identity to disguise my own identity. I will not force false names of invention on them. Instead, I will wait until they blossom with their own names. I will respectfully include in my poetry only as much as it reveals to me.

In conclusion, I pray that my creation of poetry will long remain with me as my training of the mind, my science, and my worship.

Poems from *Liking in Silence* (2006)

Depth of a Landscape

The wind blows,
short blades of grass shiver and tremble,
yet no one pays attention.

With the lonely trembling,
one moment in the life of those tender things,
one evening of the universe finally fades into night.
Between this side and that of the trembling,
between the first and last moment, is the infinitely old stillness
of ancient times, or maybe a young stillness
belonging to a time yet to come,
smeared faintly, scarcely visible
in the spring sunlight of that listless stillness.
I long to fall sound asleep for one or two hundred years,
or three months and ten days at least.
And beside my infinity, my three months or ten days,
butterflies or bees, insects with nothing much to brag about
may heedlessly brush past;
as if in a dream.
I think I shall recognize a familiar scent borne on those tiny creatures'
feelers or wings or tiny legs
as your gaze, grown deeper in some other lifetime.

Homeless

Removing your clothes like old newsprint
I lay you, raw, on a damp quilt and look down at you.
Your gnarled hands and feet have lost their vigor,
the traces of thin limbs and ribs, how weary they look.
I'm sorry.
I earned a living using you,
got a woman and built a home.
All that's left are stale sweat and a road to nightmares.
Once again, I lay you down, docile,
in a hushed corner of an unfamiliar place.
What else could I do?
I'm not saying there were no good days,
but it was a long way before you received
even a wretched wage for your labors.
I wonder if I should simply go quietly away,
leave you sleeping here like this.
How about it, body?

Cosmos Flowers

You empty pockets
of one who never persecuted anyone!

When shall we go back home
and, weeping, relate to father
all that has happened since we left?

One Spring Night

"When I die, you'll donate at least fifty thou', won't you, old brother? Nowadays a lot of people only pay thirty thou', but for me, you've got to give at least fifty; you will, won't you? Sure?" A phone call from roughneck Lee Something (age 47), sloshing about in pungent waves of drink, one spring night.

"Here, I got red-bean buns, you've got to eat them while they're hot." Screaming like he's swallowed a train, poet Park Something (age 47) barges into the middle of the quiet gathering and hands over a plastic bag. "Give me a kiss, one kiss!" He thrusts out a face black from drinking, one spring night.

"At any rate, we have to be clear about marking our beginning and end, fellas!" Jang (age 51), the owner of a chicken-and-carp-soup restaurant fusses. "To start, let's sing the national anthem. "Aigo, it's the first time such a fine song has ever been heard at our place!" the halfwit barmaid (age 50) remarks, pouring on and on, even the leftover wine she's grabbed from an empty table, one spring night.

"It's a hundred twenty thousand won really, but I'll just take a hundred thousand." So with an "Are you sure?" they fumble through wallets, finally putting fifty thousand on the slate; then, with a "Still, let's have just one more," they wave index fingers, pulling one another by the sleeve to a streetside cart-bar, one spring night.

Death, too, erupts as a crimson rash.
Kang Something, Kim Something, O Something, they've all gone on ahead.
I, too, would rather drift off to some southern streamside
and fall without a care like a graceless magnolia blossom,

needing another fifty thousand won
for reasons this and that, one night.

Someone Who Makes a Bridge Feel Lonely

God,
suppose I took a poem like this
and worked hard to transcribe it again—
couldn't you consider that as writing a new poem?

I see someone crossing a bridge.
He walks, stops briefly, and looks at the distant hills,
walks, pauses, and does the same again.

A little later someone else crosses the bridge.
Passing with quick steps, he's soon gone without a trace.
Only the bridge he's crossed remains alone, empty.

Someone quickly crossing a bridge makes the bridge feel lonely.

That's how the poem goes.
(There are plenty of other good poems, you say?)

If you say it won't do, well, it can't be helped.
But please, God,
don't make a poem feel lonely
by passing through it too fast.

Have I looked at the stars too much,
Have the stars been soiled?
Have I looked at the sky too much?
Has the sky been soiled?

He's a trembling spirit who's quit this world.

Encounter with a Little Toe

The moment I noticed the little toe enclosed in a stocking, I sobered up in a flash. Lying upside-down with downcast eyes in the body's most secluded corner, it embodied a million years of human history, so I dared not even hover about it with sentimental adjectives such as 'pitiful' or 'pathetic.' From those starving in Afghanistan to the wife of my father's second cousin who was a comfort woman for the Japanese army, it seemed that enshrined within its subdued modesty were the spirits of wounds from time immemorial.
Seized with a moment's dread that the bent, hidden thing might have died, my hand involuntarily reached down and nudged it.
Ah, see how it shrinks back, saying it's alive!
That response brought tears to my eyes, as it somehow felt like a hopeless symbol of our hope.
The woman sitting with her back to me, maybe or maybe not sensing what I was feeling, drew her foot in slightly, pulled down the hem of her skirt, and gently covered it over.

The Way Back Home

Amidst thundering traffic
a yellow dog trails endlessly
along the edge of a city freeway.

Will it get back home alive?

Exposed beneath the curled-up tail,
its rosy ass.

Jeonju

Walking slowly, pushing my bicycle
along a riverside path one summer's evening
is a fairly refreshing activity.
At the end of the embankment,
I'll put all my dark thoughts down
and have fish stew at Hwasun restaurant
with a good slug of soju.
But wishing to avoid spending today
I go to the water's edge, look for minnows,
then turn back, deliberately staggering as if drunk.
Quite good!
Poplar leaves shimmer in the evening light,
the smooth breeze slips under my loosened shirt
(such luxuries!),
my feet press firmly on the ground.
Shoulders and hips gently sway.
My stomach feels full and contented.
Should pennies be pinched beyond shady back-alleys?
Only
only this is Jeonju's riverside.
Late summer. Air and water are pure,
the path where I push my bicycle is lined with willows.
On such an evening,
perhaps a friend living in the Pole Star will come visit,
mounted on a stout-bellied donkey.
If so, I'll meet him beyond Gugil restaurant
in front of Hwanggeum general store.
He on his donkey, I pushing my bicycle, wheels squeaking as they turn,
we'll go to my house with its spacious *maru* on Gyodong hill,
laughing uproariously,
this breeze-blessed evening.

Rain

Drizzle drifting, drizzle drifting,

drizzle drifting behind that fellow drifting off,

drizzle drifting too

over the poplar's indifferent trunk;

you grew old before you reached twenty

and the ocean's still far away.

Drizzle drifting away, gaunt back turned,

drifting winter drizzle,

there's no catching you, withering drifting drizzle.

Buried in the Sea at Yerae

When I shut my eyes, I can see a white sea.
Was your naked body proud of your flushed face?
Will you believe that I ground my teeth, longing for you?
Will you believe that I bit my nails, to no avail, to no avail?
Ashamed of my advanced age,
I casually pass, watching you from the corner of my eye.
What shall I do?
You are childish, my mouth brims with the taste of sour apricots,
my body grows feverish as an unchaste young monk's;
shall I, trembling, say: I want you, I want you?
Ah, goddammit, I'm the guy who cast his heart away.
Before your dazzling purity,
I swallow my hidden tears like a wounded animal
and my sickness only grows worse.

Late Autumn 1

I weep for that woman in pain over lost love.
Now past forty,
her knuckles have thickened;
exhausted from worry, her face has collapsed.

Love waits,
hidden beneath a chestnut tree
in late autumn's bleak half-light.
A man always staggers past
in the midst of a drunken rout.
Bracing herself against the soaking chill,
she hesitantly moves her white rubber shoes
to match his steps further ahead.

Awaking, rising late at night
when all the world is still,
she washes her hair.
Under a weak lamp, no one coming, no one going,
she simply rubs her hands in silence.

Near a Firing Range

A pheasant calls. A turtle dove coos.
Pine trees stand idle, heads laden with cones.
The forest looks tender green, innocent
as a twelve-year-old Iraqi girl. Amidst the ruins
there is tenderness in thick brows and large eyes, too.
Is that an ancient weariness or a death-like despair?
The pheasant calls again. Wretched thing.
With neither hatred nor pity, just speechlessly,
those Americans, Bush and Rumsfeld, come to my mind.
Are their pine trees tender green too? Signifying what?
The pheasant calls, speechless, not a real call, just a squawk.
Are there pheasants in the land of the 12-year-old girl and her young father?
The air is full of flies.
They're like third-grade school kids let loose on a playground.
We have to put up with children.
But there's no hope in blatant ignorance.
I unwillingly recall department stores where things must be expensive
to sell; a former president claiming 290,000 won was all he owned,
television, professional sports, and the like.
Breaking the silence, a bird bursts forth.
Whatever, it's all good. (No, it's not good).
I have no intention of blaming anyone after all this time.
We are beginning to resemble the thing
we have long been dreaming of together in harmony
(for example, pigs or hyenas).
As ever, the plants wear innocent, languid expressions,
the ants run about, this way and that,
but they don't look so very greedy.
A cigarette butt, thrown away long ago,
lies amongst them, soiled, as though part of the family.
A pheasant calls.

Writings of the Dead

Writings left behind are melancholy as orphans.

After signing their names, clearly, with calloused fingers,

which universe have they scattered to?

A winter's night,

the sound of a bucket falling deep into a well.

Gunha-ri in Winter

Ash-hued roads pass
between abandoned houses
Trees stand along the roadside
like abandoned brooms.
Beneath neglected walls
Sunchang pepper paste's red tubs,
black plastic bags, and scraps of styrofoam
lie half-buried in the ground.
At the end of the wall, pushing open a forsaken door,
a bent over old man in a fur-lined jacket appears.
He's slowly going somewhere.
An abandoned dog sways after him.
The butcher's door beside the barbershop opens briefly;
someone splashes water into the street, closes the door.

The dust-pale canvas door of the store lifts
and a youthful soldier in army green
clutching a five-pack of ramen, smile aglow,
cuts across the crossroad.

End of Mourning

After setting up the photo of the deceased,
piling up rice cakes, meat, pancakes,
arranging fruit according to category and color,
taking the lid off the rice, inserting the spoon into it,
tapping three times with the chopsticks,
reading the memorial prayer,

the seven-year-old chief mourner
bows and offers a cup of wine,
the haggard widow bows tearfully
and offers a cup of wine, the younger brother bows,
a few friends bow,
the youngest sister offers a cup of wine.
Outside the darkness
is heavy with misty rain.

By now, beneath the ground, your flesh
must already have begun to rot.
Off you go on your journey.
This is your last meal,
eat your fill,
get drunk, then totter off
on your journey. Off you go.

Nobody Knows

Where have all my old earths gone?
Where have that yard, those paths gone, moist even in sunlight?
Where have my old streams gone, with their sun-baked gravel?
Where has my old hill gone, with the will-o'-the-wisps that rolled in
with night?
Where have the neighborhood elders gone, dignified even in undershirts
and pajamas? Where have all my sisters gone, with their flowery laughter?
Where have my hungers gone? Where has the sharp smell of young
green eggplants gone?
My once youthful mother with her many griefs,
my brothers with their hard calves, where have they all dispersed?
Where have my old fivestones and marbles gone, the broom that beat my
spine, my father's powerful forearms, the gloating girl next door?
Where have all my old graves gone, the pale pasqueflowers and pottery
shards I used to play with?
Where have my old spring evenings gone? The foxtails growing under the
tall poplars, the low chimney stacks, the languid eventide smoke?
Where has my cramped, dark room gone? My dark grandfather, his dark
coughing and the dark wicker trunks, where have they dispersed?
Where has the old me gone? Down what streets did I wander, dispersed, a
child with dirt-black feet emerging from rubber shoes?

At Yeongweol

What are they waiting for? Every year
mountains crane their necks, trees stand idle,
Where do the tinted sands go each night to collapse?
Does it sink completely in
once darkness has crossed?
What are they waiting for,
that they wander, rustling like wind, over the plains,
only to return each morning?

Unless it's expectation,
why would they remain?
Unless it's expectation,
would flesh dry up and skin shrivel?
Unless it's expectation,
how could they even die?

What are they waiting for?

Completely forgetting
that being here at Yeongweol,
where all the roads have been paved,
is expectation,
Whose sleep am I sleeping in their place?
Whose food am I eating in their place?
Whose walk am I walking in their place?

Friends

Living rough

They're poorly dressed loafers without valid credit cards.
Wearing old parkas, they gather together
wondering who to annoy next,
mischief already twinkling in their eyes.
These loafers even play cards with their mouths running.
Thrilled by a game of paduk with five thousand won at stake,
they laugh themselves silly.
The spectators laugh too.
Beside themselves, they roll around
on the floor above the stove boiling cattle-feed,
roasting their backs with laughter.
They grow warm inside from downing one another
like a serving of well-boiled scorched rice.

They'll turn up again today with matted beards and unkempt hair.
Giving off the stench of cigarettes, they'll gather
like bohemians of old in this dim corner.

Remembered Disgrace

A radiant young woman resembling filmstar Jeon Ji-Hyeon is approaching,
walking on crutches with incomparable vitality (but walking on crutches) in
a skirt, high heels, a jade-hued scarf. The sky clear (something strange, still).

The right high heel is missing.
The right stocking is missing.
The right calf, knee, thigh are missing.

I brush past.
I cannot look back.

I wonder,
does life still have manners?

A Secret Incident

One evening, pleased with neither this nor that
a prematurely dead leaf drops stealthily beside me.

Beside me, there where I can only simply be,
it too is simply there, saying nothing.

Thanks!
Really, this is something to be grateful for.

Depth of a Landscape 2

This road, along which someone without anything in the world to lean on
    passed by weeping and carrying a small bundle,
this road turned sorrowful,
with oak trees and spicebush, dog-rose and pasqueflowers, young weeds,
    empty now, where not one animal passes all day long,
a bright, dark road.

That person set out at age seventeen,
drifted about, finally squatted as an old cobbler at Jochiwon Market,
his hands slowly sewing and polishing,
eating soup with rice alone every evening
in a small restaurant at the alley's end,
once in a while, staring into the distance over his reading glasses,
his face,
a quiet, dark road.

Homeless 2

They have bodies but no space in which to unburden them. They have
no space they can use, no space to eat and die. So
where can they put their feet, put their head, the mouth that eats, the stomach
that contains, the anus that excretes, where can they put them?
Their shit,
where can they deposit it?
Because all their spaces have been confiscated, they
cannot exist,
thus their lives cannot blossom. Like naphthalene
or a ghost, it is boiled down alive, then evaporated.
So their time merely comes and goes like a splash of dirty water
staining a streetside wall or innocent trouser-hems.
Where have all those honorable spaces gone? Have they really
swallowed up all those fresh spaces? As the rumors say,
were those good spaces shit on, then removed?
They exist in negative space as antimatter.
If those in space look at those in no-space,
they don't exist. Once stolen space is returned, they must not be.
So their present lies only in disgorging,
in turning themselves inside out.
So they vomit. Vomit their throat, their guts, their anus, all the worthless
stuff beyond the anus, Tom, Dick and Harry, petty quarrels, bitter tears,
finally vomiting their mouth itself.
With their innards turned inside out from mouth to anus,
they are there, pretending to be there, grimly earnest;
they are a black hole, at once completion and death. All space forfeited.

We are stuck above their guts.
We are vomited up in the space they have vomited up.
We are in what lies beyond their anus.

Memorial to the Filial Devotion of Lee from Gyeongju

"When her husband, Pang Sugori, died, leaving her with a daughter, she buried him in the family plot, and supported her baby and her aged mother-in-law by rice-milling and sewing. When a great nine-year drought began, she headed for the far-off southeastern region, carrying her mother-in-law on her back, to find a living. Less than a year later, after her mother-in-law died, she took the corpse on her back, walked the seven hundred li back to the family plot and buried her there. She built a hut near the grave and observed three years of grieving and mourning. Soon after this Lee from Gyeongju also died, aged forty-seven."

Beside this inscribed plaque, weeds grow thick,
high-powered cars go roaring by.
Is God still watching them?

Melancholy names!
Pang Sugori.
Lee from Gyeongju.
Her mother-in-law.

Rainy Season

Shall we go to Suta-sa temple on Mount Gongjak
to see the water celery
shall we go to see the wild pinks
on a day when rain is pouring down
shall we go to dry our wet feet
on a hot floor in the living quarters of Suta-sa
shall we go to view the distant hills through the window
on a rainy day after a rainy day after a rainy day
after beholding a peony for a good while beside a drooping ash tree
offering old Buddha a couple of bows
then if we're bored
if we are nonetheless bored shall we call
for the young daughter-in-law who's not here and play cards
or, damn it, shall we go and beg a handful of rice crusts to munch
from the temple cook
this long long rainy season

Busy, Busy

Busy, you're frightening.
Busy, you look angry.
You kick the ground hard as you walk along.
You never have a moment to thank your toes, heels, the sinews in your
calves, the bones in your knees.
You never have a moment to tell your legs, your feet, your shoes, the
ground, the wind: "There's urgent work to be done; I know it may
be tough but please bear with me."
You're simply busy. And, busy, you're frightening.

Like someone rearing back for an uppercut, your neck and shoulders are taut.
Finally you lay an uppercut.
People with broken noses and cracked jaws will weep. Your fingers and
arms will ache..
But you have no time to apologize to your fist. You're busy with important
things,
you can't find a moment to think about the insult to the man you struck,
the sorrow of his poor wife, his uneducated father and brothers,
his dirty kids, because you have to make the world a safer place.
To tell the truth,
the world shakes according to how busy you are, and since the more restless
the world the busier you become,
you will never run out of pretexts for being busy.
And your busyness too will never end.

How difficult being busy is. How confident it is, too.
To be busy, how busily you have to strive. How frighteningly you have to strive.
Saying you're busy is a lonely thing but luckily you don't know how to cry.
You're so busy it wouldn't do for you to hear the nightjar crying in the woods.
It wouldn't do for you to see the celandines on springtime hills.
It wouldn't do for you to hear your old mother snoring faintly.
Since grief, peace and rest are like germs gnawing away at a busy soul,

food simply exists to be devoured, breath simply to be breathed away.

Today again you're just busy
and your busy eyes are vicious.
I wonder how hard a time the two walnuts between your busily-moving
legs must be having without knowing why, and I feel rather sorry for them.

Hwajin

When a typhoon comes,
her heart will flutter
like a young street girl's.
When the wind penetrates her flesh
and the distant sky billows like a sail,
the old mule that I am
will make his way to Hwajin.
I will await the herd of elephants, the shoal of whales
sweeping over in swelling tides.
The erupting body fluids, the heavy breathing,
Hwajin, her whole body open to welcome a new man,
Hwajin, standing at the very center of that compassionate name,
the old man that I am will glow like a ball of flame.
I will ruffle my shabby mane and shudder.
Finally I, too, will make that sea.

"A Girl Hunched by the Fire Making Dough Flakes Soup—I Will Be Her Man"

That girl hunched by the fire making dough flakes soup—
dependent on her ruddy, frozen hands,
I'll end up wasting my life.
That girl with nowhere to go
only whimpers, crying alone, can't even run away.
She looks wretched, burned by the sun,
but her breasts and thighs must be whiter than milk.
Sprawled across that body, I'll wake up late, bleary-eyed,
wipe my sticky eyes with my thick, droopy beard.
At dawn, I'll rush over to the gambling room in the tavern.
I'll snoop around for leftover drinks,
flirt idly with the aging barmaid,
and once I'm drunk, I'll fall over and squander another day.
"I'm going now," I'll toss into the void a goodbye that no one hears,
then stumble home carrying starlight on my back.
When ten to twenty years have gone by like that
I'll have feebly spawned three or four children in her body.
After spawning them I'll be helpless.
That young woman
only whimpers, nowhere to go.
The children will grow up rough as badgers.
Lying in a dirt-floored room as dark as a cave,
my head resting on my arm,
I'll watch snow flutter in through a crack in the fogged window.
Puffing bitter cigarettes, I'll let more years go by.
When that woman's waist grows thick, her tears run dry
and her eyes blaze blue flames,
I'll suddenly fall badly sick and make my bed under a rack.
I'll hide the liquor she doesn't want me to have and keep drinking doggedly.
When her hair is half white from years of hardship

at long last I'll expire ahead of her.
By then she won't be able to laugh or cry.
She'll smoke the bitter cigarettes I used to smoke,
learn to drink the liquor she couldn't handle, learn to swear.

Wouldn't this be quite a hopeless love?
I'm not sure if it makes any sense.

Has Love Come?

Is this a dream? What kind of dream could this be?
Over there, all alone,
bearing death-like darkness front and back,
one flawed lotus blossom.
Could a single lotus blossom unexpectedly rise up, white?
Has love come? (Aigu, really! Pitiful!)
But that waxen face and those sodden long tresses—
could it be Simcheong who drowned? That very Simcheong,
dead and now returning?
Across those dark waters of death,
an orchid swollen with water.

To see one's child at seventy!
(Aigu, really!)

Belated Love

After lingering long in one corner of my sky
a bird
departs.

Red toes
loosely curled together,
white brow.

It's like a neatly written message
left by someone who died.

The sky is empty, deserted!

I suppose I shall grow old
pointlessly snooping from house to house,
dragging old shoes with the heels scuffed down.

Thaw

Beyond Deer Pass and over Mount Simhak
lies Jogang Landing.

Between bare-skinned piers that braved the winter
snow drifts down
white splinters of ice

and perched on them,
heads held proudly high like Jeon Bong-jun,

do-or-die,
do-or-die, floating down,
a black flock of mallard ducks.

Springtime Sea

The village head's wife
had a big behind,
as big as a tub,
as big as a tub.

The village head's wife
was big-bosomed, too,
the front of her worn vest
as big as a grave-mound.
as big as a grave-mound.

How I longed to lie like rose-moss
beside her as she dozed.
How I longed to sink
into her faint snoring.

How I longed to be reborn
as her third son,
sleek and good-looking,
go to Seoul and set up with a wealthy widow.

Deokpyeong Market

His mere three fingers are embarrassed.
Holding packs of cotton balls and disposable bandages,
he shouts, *One thousand won!*
But buyers are few.
His eyes sting in the blazing sun.

Widow Yun from the acorn jelly shop shouts: *Come have a bite to eat!*
With brisk wet hands
she serves up acorn-jelly.
Kim from the rummage sale charges out from the Co-op Bank
        rattling his moneybelt.
His hands hold seasoned chicken feet and soju.
Business must be booming.
He continues to fuss while wiping sweat from beneath his visor.
After a few swigs pour down his parched throat, he gets drowsy.

Knowing she won't take them,
he holds out a couple bills.
He studiously ignores Widow Yun's bright arms and breast,
his mutilated hand bashful as it retracts.

Suppose I take some Dorco sets or toothbrushes to market tomorrow?
The sun is still high.

One thousand won a pack!
He suddenly raises his voice.

Late Autumn 2

Silly rain sprinkles down on the walnut leaves

The legs of the stalking stork stalking grow longer still.

How about having a bite of cold rice soaked in water,
then going to dry persimmons at the neighbors' house?

Pushing up her reading-glasses,
mother is darning socks.

But where on earth will the grasshoppers
find shelter from this rain?

Butterfly

An approaching butterfly—
what can that be on its back?
I don't know; a scrap of waning midday's lonely shadows
in a courtyard's corner, the corner of an empty house?
Could it be the weeping of a child left alone,
dribbling out
the rice and kimchi soup he's eaten?
Could it be a weeping like layers of grime trickling down,
accumulating on the chin, on the front hem?
Bearing on its back a midday no one looks after, piercing loneliness,
as it goes. How far on earth
are you going, butterfly?

There were days
when I felt like silently kneeling down before it.

Thirty Years, He Mumbles

—30th High School Reunion

Thirty years! Startled by his own voice
he wakes with a jolt from a dream:
Pack the military drill uniform, prepare a lunchbox,
it's time to get moving.

What a lifelike dream!
Dream of setting off for Seoul or elsewhere, becoming a student; dream of landing a job; dream of learning about liquor and smokes, and women, too; dream of moving around, lodging, boarding, tutoring, rotting for three years in the army; dream of studies abroad, groveling; dream of returning, finding a sweet-eyed woman and getting married; dream of setting up house together; dream of having a baby with her; dream of the child growing up; dream of fretting about the children getting into college; dream of an unsatisfying work life; dream of a late promotion; dream of making a killing on the stock exchange; dream of losing it again; dream of running away; dream of weeping alone; dream of parents falling sick; dream of who gets taken first; dream of a family row over caretaking the remaining parent; dream of staying together for the children's sake; dream of moving into a bigger place; dream of getting a bigger car; dream of struggling to entertain, play golf; dream of taking early retirement one day; then, then, dream of the wife departing first; dream of departing myself, leaving behind the wife and kids; dream of receiving an invitation to the 30th class reunion; dream of hearing my wife complaining, "Why do they want you to pay so much?" while my heart drifts off, thinking: "Has it already been that long."

As he stands in front of the cold mirror, mumbling, *Thirty years,*
beyond the thinning hair, beyond the wrinkles, far away,
he's clutching a bag stuffed with Principles of Mathematics I,
        and Comprehensive English,
he's running, youthful, with a buzz-cut, face flushed red.

As he quietly repeats, *Thirty years,*
the scent of fresh peppermint seems to rise in the pit of his stomach,
with a whiff of well-fermented salted fish,
along with the scent of a grim evening's bitter shot of soju and regret;
a smell of dried pepper-stalks burning seems to come wafting.

The buzz-cut youth in the mirror
darting into the classroom, dodging tardiness by a finger's breadth—
there's no telling if his early morning dream
has left him happy or sad.

Desperately

It's raining; the drink's going to his head; feeling sick, he's breaking into a cold sweat. It's raining and he yearns to fling his body down if only there were a dry corner. But why do his eyes keep going dim? His hands hold an umbrella and a bag, and his body keeps slumping forward. It's raining, raining, his body's limp like a wet sheet of paper, and in his memories rise faint shadows of old friends, which pass like a magic lantern show, leaving sharp cuts in his heart. Carrying an umbrella in one hand, a bag with unidentifiable contents in the other, desperately, there being no other suitable posture, desperately, water seeps into his shoes and the traffic signal seems like it's never going to change.

Cockscomb

Broken Cockscomb.
Broken-backed cockscomb !
It's the stone-walled path where sweet-voiced Na Hun-a
regretfully turned away.
Beyond the jujube tree's drooping branches,
the sky has frozen an ashen gray.
Nearly decapitated?
Broken back!
More wretched than a stumpy broom,
tossed into the corner in an ashery,
your crimson comb that dazzled for a season
bleeds now as it sweeps the ground.
Neck more wretched than a tattered ad flyer
blowing about after the market's closed,
that neck, soaked through,
the winter rain unceasing,
and no one is looking out the window.
Cockscomb.

Rice

In a flash I sober up.
A lump forms in my throat as I remember those I left behind.

I silently polish off of a bowl of rice!

There beside it,
I finally pull my scattered self together.
Straining to open drooping eyes, I kneel,
my heart swells.
Oh, I am indeed a sinful man.
Beyond the mound of white rice, my hometown's stream rolls on,
the arms that wielded a scythe,
old mother's narrow shoulders as she rolls over, lonely.

Where on earth have I been spilled?

That bent back, turned away, drawing on a cigarette,
one bowl of rice.

Hiding a Knife behind a Smile

Hiding a knife behind a smile,
hiding bloodshot eyes behind a wistful tone,
cowardly
cowardly
I speak of love.
Like an assassin who once crossed the Yi River,
this hidden bluster.
Whether the knife is there
no longer makes any difference.
I've quite forgotten whether it is.

An Empty Room

I'll lie down now.
Spring plants are fading before they've even flowered.
We must have come too far.
Now night is falling.

Only those frightful children with hookworms
tumble amidst the long-stalked greens;
alas, the flower fields are all destroyed.

The good sunlight of spring days,
the leaves that once rejoiced,
the gentle brows that once sat in silence around an evening meal—
beneath whose eaves are they weeping now?

I'll settle down like an old crow
on the end of a lofty branch.
Fearful days
are coming near.

Here, one glass.
Surely there are things more dolorous than liquor.
Nonetheless, one glass.

The End of the Road

A tiny weed stands in my way—
those slender veins that look
as though they will burst at a touch.
A drop of rain stands in my way.

Things already committed!
Mistakes completed!

Those thick leaden skies that, however hard we try,
seem to belong to someone else.
Names I once briefly loved.

What body shall I be granted now?
In what moonlight will my soles and my kneecaps,
flattened by sorrow, dry white?

Acacia

Does fragrance come from a distant star?
Were there days, indeed, when we
rolled like two gentle animals on that star?
I don't remember,
Acacia.

Empty countenance!
Blue veins on the back of your hands,
little sister in the village I left behind.

To a Dried Mugwort Stalk

Dried mugwort stalk!
Loose flurries of snow
one winter's evening dusk!

Your mother's grave lies far away.
Do you know that,
dried mugwort?

You can't have forgotten
the dark shade of the walnut tree,
your fretting little sister with her worm-scabbed head
your friends with all those warts on the backs of their hands . . . .

We ought to make ancestral offerings,
we ought to make ancestral offerings.

A poor family's eldest grandson, prematurely dead.
Dried mugwort stalk!

A Summer's Day

The plants grow without hurry, without worry—
brothers, sisters-in-law,
mothers-in-law, nieces, all mingled together,
so idle is a summer's midday.

Balsam, rose moss, marvel-of-Peru, geranium,
lilies, chilis are blossoming—
sisters and brothers, they blossom together.

A hen followed by a few scruffy chicks
makes a grand tour of the neighborhood.

I sit there with one of my peep-peeping offspring.
On a rare summer's day after the rain has cleared,
I watch them without hurry, without worry.
Such is life, such is life. Eyes sting.

Off to New York

Our daughter and her cousins
board a flight for New York,
little by little it leaves the ground, takes off.
Through the palm-sized window she waves
goodbye, calling out, *Mummy! Daddy!*
The parents left behind, wave and shout
every time they see their children's faces at the window.
Have a safe journey. Write to us!

They see how they peer out seeking mummy's and daddy's faces
every time they come round,
Haigo-ya! and quite fittingly so,
nose tingling, heart chilly.
Then stealthily fear sneaks in.
Those children who insist on taking flights for New York, Paris,
rather than for Busan or Seoul,
will one day really leave for New York or Paris,
and suppose they don't come back?
Imagine how we'll feel then.

Impossible to give voice to it, but I worried
as I watched our daughter
riding on a 500-won-a ride
airplane roundabout
at Geumgang Park in Busan.

A Lucid Sound

The chief monk of Deokwon stole an armlet
with nine jujube beads and gave it to me;
ding, ding, ding, a lucid sound
seemed to ring in my heart,
so I kept it in my pocket.
Whenever I met a girl,
whenever I drank liquor,
I fingered it.

It's been some time
since I've heard any sound.
Have I (Right on!),
become a dog of a man?

Buried Deep

In everyone's heart
there's a vast, empty ocean.

In everyone's heart,
there's a lingering, poignant song,
the twisted shadow of a wild pear tree.

In everyone's heart,
there are faces frozen with fear,
and bloodshot eyes.

In everyone's heart,
there hides a blind alley, a sharp sickle,
a blue flame.

In everyone's heart,
there's a bamboo grove where autumn rain patters down.

The Night before the Lunar New Year

I pour down another glassful.
The liquor glides past my tongue, my mouth, my uvula,
pursuing its path inside my body.
It seems to be saying that it, too, is no longer naive
like it used to be in the old days.

Hot and bitter.

The innkeeper curled up
at the far end of the room
already seems to be dreaming of going home.
As I pour down yet another glassful,
I quietly tell my insides:

The high threshold at Suda-sa temple is not all.
There's also a Way in the shadowy sleep of a cheap brothel.
This is good enough.

A Flower

In the merciless wind and rain
the flower at long last lay flattened.

After a night-long fever
I rise with a puffy face
and push open the window.

We must live!

Rise up, flower!
You have to feed your kids
and send them off to school.

YOL

All in vain, says the wind.
Childhood memories of an old beggar
left behind somewhere in his huddled winter dreaming.
The dawn when he woke to the smell of his mother's apron,
such a dawn has finallly
drifted far away, can be found nowhere in the world,
says the windy, snow-covered road. And now
the window of the village bus, coolly against his brow,
rattles and agrees that nothing remains on this unending road.

The world has changed,
and time has passed helplessly by.
The children, grown up,
have acquired unfamiliar, dark-bearded faces
while the grown-ups have departed one by one.

Walking that snowy road of death
for ten years, a hundred years, how odd,
the road of prisons and graves and hatred.
Ah, is anyone there! Anybody there! Cry though he may,
what else could it be?
A man thickly coated in despair like you,
a man with bitter winter's icicles on his brows and beard,
holding funerals for parents, wife and children, food for the crows,
a man unable to either live or die, trapped in a body,
with nowhere to go, nowhere to stay in this land.

Like a landscape in a faded black-and-white photo
the time of that unending snow silently speaks:
Every road is imprisoned in death.
It speaks: *The roads on earth have vanished.*
If you want to go, turn into a bird and fly away.

Long Ago

I miss the dizzying smell of grass, the insect sounds,
the swish of dewdrops against our ankles
heard while pushing through the woods
along the path that summer night.
Like two naive baby fawns
our bodies flushed, ha, with our bodies flushed,
we simply moved along the rain-washed mountain path,
merely inhaled short breaths,
merely touched arms now and then, pretending it accidental,
drew close, inhaled the other's scent, pretending not to.
In the pitch dark, beneath your bound-up tresses,
the bare flesh of your neck shone, translucent.
And my hands, a mass of scratches, were lovely too.

Passing ridge after ridge,
on the hillside path behind your village
your older brother's eyes glared as he waited anxiously.
But we, two shy wild animals barely awakened from a dream,
never even held hands.
On the way back home
I screamed songs at the top of my lungs.

Injeolmi Rice Cakes

Once my maternal grandmother set off with a basin of injeolmi rice cakes
on her head,
to sell in this neighborhood and that.
I pulled out pieces of glass, bottle tops, a broken pocket knife,
medicine bottles, a fruit knife with no handle, burst beanbags,
all hidden on the sunny side of the old wattle fence behind the privy,
and played with them.
Bored of even that after half a day,
I chased the innocent chickens from the house behind,
then ended up being scolded by my youngest aunt
for scuffling my shoes along.
I ate, blowing *hoo hoo,* a bowl of sujaebi dough flakes soup, more kimchi
than dough,
mingled with tears and snot.
Humming a line or two of "Yellow Shirt" that I learned from the radio,
I collapsed on the warm floor and slept like a cat.
Then seeing the door was dim, unsure if it was morning or evening,
frightened, with one cheek bright red, I cried out
and my aunt, putting wood on the fire, pretended it was morning.
When grandmother came home at sunset,
if her business had been good, I'd be so disappointed.
I'd lick my fingertips and dip them again and again
into the fine bean powder left at the bottom of the basin
until my fingers pruned.

Ah, those injeolmi grandmother
used to stuff into my mouth, gaping
with longing for my mother!
Passing Yongsan market, I see them again, laid out on a shabby stall.
I see grandmother, huddled, dozing.

A Bird

Bird,
flown upstream
as far as this city riverside,
seagull,
your gestures are already peaceful,
you're not a thing of this world.
There is nowhere here
for you to shake your head, unfurl your wings.
Beyond your graceful wing-beats time has stopped,
only death-like stillness lies deep, so deep.

Who can know
the secret tension in the muscles, the two bloodshot eyes
that launched the body into the air?

There is nobody here
and you were so dignified.
Return and rest, bird,
before you fly into the beautiful sky of days yet to come.

On the spot where you passed,
not one persimmon flower has fallen.

At the Crossroads

Is that so?
Well, it may be.
Though I stretch, stretch out my hand
all I feel is empty air, a scrap of wind.
It may be a consuming regret
that makes me stand in agony, arms outstretched.

I don't know. It might be nothing at all.
It might be a swallow of cold water drunk after fumbling
in the dark while going home alone.
Maybe it's a senseless dream I can't seem to wake from.
Yet I'm bound to wake.
It might be a carelessly falling leaf.

But what could it be?
This thing, like crying that rises even as I look away.
This thing, making me run to it, struggling and wriggling.
This thing, making me stand in a cutting wind
leaning on an empty promise that is not a promise nor anything at all.
What could it be?

Mirror

There is a man overwhelmed with fear.
His hair is bushy as a young pine, his beard is scraggley.
I look at his pursed lips.
That man is a fugitive
and I, crying *No,* was pressed forth,
to stand face to face with him on a cliff at world's end.
Shall I extend my hand for a shake?
Oho, a handshake at least?
Just brushing past is surely better.
Fearful face.
Passing like strangers is surely better.

Old Age

Wind is blowing from far away,
the fine veins in the leaves
of the cork oak are stinging, too.

In harvested fields
flocks of birds are indifferent.

In a drawer, bought in advance,
two pairs of socks.

Maybe the kids will come home
for this year's Harvest Moon Day.

Over there, on the edge of the paddy-field,
a telephone pole.

Return to the West

"Never forget me," I sing.
To whom shall I speak about sorrow?
The stars shine bright and lonesome. To you?

The day I set off for far away,
my ties with this world were finished,
I cannot go leaving you behind
with your tendrils and pretty braids, your white neck.
Rain will fall from every cloud,
I shall writhe in tears.

Even then, I'll most likely feign indifference,
feign indifference and whistle.
Setting off, resolutely calm,
I'll not once look back
nor drop a single hair

To whom shall I speak about sorrow?
The stars shine bright and lonesome. To you?

Leaving Him Behind

The dead are dead, but the living are still alive
so we light a fire in the midst of the eleventh month.
Twigs catch fire quickly, burn in a flash,
Thick sticks burn long but catch fire slowly,
Handfuls of dry leaves blaze up.
Big branches burn lonesome, all alone.

The silently swelling grave mound
is like a nail in the heart
so we hover about, hover about,
only hover about.
The remarkable void in the aftermath of the dead fire.

Forgive us
for rummaging through our empty pockets
after burying you alone in the cold ground,
lighting a fire beside you,
fastening our clothes in the wind.
Forgive us
for going back down the hill without you,
returning home.

Public Holiday

Placing his family neatly against the railing of Chungrang Bridge
a man is taking photos.
Tanned by the sun, their faces are dark,
grinning, pouting, in high spirits, taking a family photo.
For the the rural woman carrying a child on her back,
it's the first time in her life, so she's shy and happy.
Her face flushed, she's beside herself.
The older child is pressed against her,
standing at attention as he's learned at school,
rolling his eyes as he holds his breath,
while through a gap in the railing beside him
one cosmos flower is peeking, its head extended,
and a woman, the wife's mother or the husband's, holds their things,
and bustles about telling passers-by to get out of the way.

Spring Fever

Such is life.

Such is the setting tide of time.

Nearly touching, nearly touching, never touching

In a springtime alley at nightfall

returning home rubbing empty hands.

Brother and Sister

On my way home, riding the number 57 bus,
a little girl maybe six years old boards
ahead of a boy perhaps two years older.
After presenting two tickets wriggled out of his pocket,
he grabs his sister's hand and plants it on the back of a seat,
while he barely dangles on a suspended grip.
Spotting an empty seat, he tells his sister, *Sit there!*
She pulls tensely aside
and bangs on the empty seat with her fist: *You sit here.*
I'm OK, he reassures her.
Every time the bus jerks, he looks anxiously down at her,
while she firmly grips the back of the seat with both hands
and looks up at him as if to say: *I'm doing fine, aren't I?*

I watch, pretending not to,
such a pretty sight.
On my way home from a memorial service for Mr. Chae,
who left a child behind,
where I'd vented my anger with liquor,
my eyes, that had stayed sober throughout,
on seeing them,
are filled with tears.

Yeosu

The shack's stone floor is scorching hot,
and Jeong, the mason from Suncheon, spends the day sleeping.
A winter's evening by the sea at Sinweol-dong.
Is his second son, gone to study in Gwangju,
managing his meals all right?
His body haggard,
money's not being raked in as he had hoped,
and it's another five days before low tide.
The sum on his tab keeps increasing.
The lapping sea seems to be asking for something,
the dogs run barking after the wind

Waking from sleep, Jeong faces the sea and loosens his belt.
The piss goes flying sideways.

Flower, Let's Go to the River

Flower, with hand on your brow.
Flower, with gaunt hand on your brow.

Let's go to the darkly flowing river's edge
The lips of baby pebbles are blue with cold,
the rough calves of water peppers in clusters.

Let's go to the river together,
and once at the river
let's simply look at the water.

Stars filling the sky will shine bright in the heavens.
Frost will be white on the bent backs of wilting grass.

As if drunk, as if in sorrow, let's go to the river,
let's just silently look at the water.
Flower, with hand on your brow.

Poems from

Beside a Baby Donkey

(2015)

A Snail

I've always wondered about the inside of the ear.

I've heard that there's a snail living in there.
Starved for outside sounds, it must have paved that lonely path.
Mouth pressed to the path's end,
it must have quenched its thirst with the few sounds
          that managed to get through.
If not a snail's home, then
it might have been the bandit's cave my sister was carried off to in olden days,
or my blind maternal grandfather's tiny room,
though once past that shameful hole,
anyone would have become a snail.

But inside there, the snail
is said to have gone on a journey, promising
          to return in a thousand years or so.
After the ear has died,
after all who are curious about the inside of the ear have vanished,
after every path has crumbled,
every sound and thirst have come to an end,
it's said to travel on through the long, long years,
crawling along infinitely, slowly,
four horns erect in solitude
like the emblem of some ruined kingdom,
fumbling its way blindly
along a far-reaching path.

Flat Against the Wall

A bent back
collects newpapers, folds up empty boxes and ties them together,
workpants much too baggy for a shriveled eighty-year-old.
The moment a car enters the alleyway,
she stands flat against the wall,
holding on to her little cart as if it were her only child.

Lonely, standing flat against the wall
like a spider against dirty cement,
like an aged stingray on the bottom of a fish tank,
            against the gray wall
humbly, so humbly standing flat

Once the car has passed,
the old woman slowly unfolds again
like a crumpled sheet of paper.
The two wheels of her cart
follow close at her heels like two young goats

When I think of the old Samsung television
            turned on in her room in late evening,
the listing sink and the pans,
when I think of the bent back that will stand in front of them
I feel a lump in my throat.
When I think of the rag tightly squeezed and wrung out
in one corner of the room.

Mokpo

"The boats can't leave,"
so I lie face down on the warmest part of the floor in the inn,
listening half-asleep to the sound of a boat chugging off.
I imagine the seagulls, screaming and wheeling by its sides.
White, round belly and two red feet.
Leaving behind those white, round, red things,
the boat in my drowsiness chugs off following an unseen path
toward the open sea with its finely shattering sunlight.

I wonder if my old sweetheart is doing well this winter.
Perhaps she's rummaging through old drawers, wearing baggy pants and
lying on her white, round belly, watching television,
perhaps she's bending back her white neck, laughing,
revealing the inside of her red lips.
Memories sweet and smooth as a seagull's descent.
My wife would give me hell if she knew.
Unable to take it any longer, she'd put down her spoon
and slam the door behind her, no doubt; still,
my dear wife, is it so reprehensible to wonder as one ages
how an old sweetheart might be?

Outside, there's too much wind for the boats to leave.
At the foot of Mt. Yudal the tablecloth-sized window is still with sunlight.
I open a waterway through such bright drowsiness.
I must at least make it to the silver magnolia grove on Ui-do island
across the dazzling sky, the wintery sea.
I must take the chugging boat and sail, if only once,
across that midst of sleep, ever firmer now with my thickened girth.
Even if my nose and ears freeze crimson.

Galactic Communications

—On an escalator

How much weight we've gained! You and I, both.
Where did we go wrong?
Arriving on this remote
galactic star,
haunting muddy alleyways like nightmares,
thirty years,
forty years,
no, fifty years!

—*Which star did you come from?*
I ponder, amidst an unfamiliar silence
    like the 'eyes right' during a military inspection parade.
Fat, I gaze painfully at
fat you, the trim on your old overcoat, the worn-down heels of your shoes.
What brought us here, only to blow us up in so unlovely a manner?
What is it that blew us up, only to throw us aside, leaving us crumpled?
—*What kind of boy were you on that star?*
another you asks silently from behind me.
Have we met before somewhere?
This machine carrying us upward is another silent, lonely beast.
In a moment, on reaching the top, we will all scatter again, fast.
Returning to our muddy alleyways,
we'll be fathers licking their fingers to count money,
aged fathers slurping down rice and soup.

We won't remember, you and I,
this odd, brief moment.
Nor will the stars we left behind remember us.
Will we be able to find a ticket back? With this sluggish body
I dread the time spent waiting on some star beyond the murky sky.
How do you feel?

There is No Fighting against Such Odds.

After contributing a few cents toward a nephew's schooling,
my children's tuition fees are a squeeze.
To pay the interest on the credit union account, I charge it on this card,
and use that card to pay off what's due on this one.
Then rolls around the eightieth birthday of my folks in the countryside,
and a few days after,
my mother-in-law is hospitalized for arthritis. Again,
I make the car payment, pay the phone bill,
the installment on a credit card cash advance, when
news of an aunt's death after long illness arrives. Returning
from a condolence visit, I come home
to find the wife crying,
saying her brother's bankrupt and has lost his house.

Chopsticks, two, pen, one . . . . There is no fighting against such odds,

I write in conclusion, when
a fine for unpaid parking fees flies in,
my daughter returns from the dentist in tears,
three teeth have to be extracted.
My heart sinks as I ask: *How much?*
She flares up: *How should I know?*

Mr. Jeon of the Chinese Restaurant

Suppose I could pull noodles as swiftly as he can,
wrinkling big eyes and smiling wistfully at the snotty-nosed kids peeking in,
tall and shambling along with head thrust forward,
untying the dirty apron and disdainfully throwing it crumpled into a corner,
talking in a strange accent, like Mr. Jeon of the Chinese restaurant.

As for future hopes, I wouldn't mind becoming president or a general,
I wouldn't mind becoming a wealthy businessman or a pilot, but he

was dazzling, Mr. Jeon of the Chinese restaurant who chewed gum so well,
every time he moved his lips they made a clacking noise,
when he whistled
the passing girls were sure to giggle.
He once caught a snake by the neck with his bare hands.

One autumn he got beaten up by Mr. Kim from uptown
and wept, his nose bleeding, that widower Mr. Jeon.
Though I didn't want to be like the ragged undershirt, sorrowful ribs,
though I didn't want to be like his little son,
          who followed him and wept behind a pillar
(though I followed suit and wept a bit too).

At about the time cherry blossoms fell
Mr. Jeon from China disappeared with his little son.
With the lady from the cosmetics shop?
With the daughter of the shop owner?

Did he take the road back to his own star?
Has he started another Chinese restaurant there,
          chewing gum in his undershirt,
skillfully pulling noodles?
My childhood idol, Mr. Jeon of the Chinese restaurant.

The Prime of Life

The good days drift away, like a lost scarlet hair pin, like the falling evening tide. Good days leak away between the fingers like grains of sand, pointless like the word *pointless,* futile like the word *futile.* The beard turns gray, wicked time squats on the corners of the eyes and tugs. Before we know it, dust settles on every windowpane and everything blurs. Where did we let go of the string? Nobody has tugged us from the other end for some time. Nobody looks at us with shining eyes.

Blind, deaf time will soon come like a winter forest, a time when nothing heartbreaking is approaching.

Farewell, farewell, tearful days,
huddled together under a small umbrella, kicking up spray with flowery boots,
setting off for a land without sorrows
live on like reckless siblings
unknown to anyone.

Round Back

Brushing a few stray hairs back behind the ears,
slowly going past the shops,
slowly past the seesaw in the playground,
past the cat by the garbage can—
a slightly bent back goes past,
a gentle back.
On that back not even a baby bird will get hurt.
A falling persimmon
doesn't burst on it but rolls down.
A warm back unknown to others,
a back you long to be quietly lulled on,
desolate heart drawn within,
offering a gentle hill to the world,
walks on slowly, the body growing smaller bit by bit.
Before long,
a round grave mound.

Where even early snow falls and briefly rests.

Bak Yeong-geun

So fearful, he would drink again and again;
so steeped in liquor that hands and feet and face were scorched and withered, black as an old spider, he longed to be carried out of the world by a breath of wind, like a wisp of straw, while everyone was asleep.

On one dark remote night back then,
camellias from Seonun-sa temple would have fallen, covering their eyes,

Please receive him gently, with both hands.
If there be a dry, sinless ground, allow him to rest a while.
He simply wishes to endure, one way or another, things like the plaintive back of a monk's head, young tender green leaves, and spring nights when apricot blossoms fall.

Foolish Desert

Weary of the dazzling autumn light, you made your way around it.
Riding a postman's old bicycle you'd stolen,
speeding merrily down a rainbow road one moonlit night,
    (Hurrah! Acting silly, butt held high)
you went off to visit the nearby old man God's village, where drunken
    bugs are rumored to exist.
Walking down a soft brick road
to that crabby old man whose white sideburns give him an advantage,
you've gone to ask him for a wager on a game of chess.

Wearing a turban that resembles the ring round the moon, bearing a load
    of baby hippos, hedgehogs, goats, old camels,
crossing the foolish desert like an idiot
you've set off in style like a prince.
The autumn sunlight is quietly bright
(Just between the two of us, I suppose all the old pros are there—Kim Jong-sam, Cheon Sang-byeong, Bak Yong-nae? I'm jealous. If ever guys like Chae Gwang-seok or Bak Yeong-geun come clamoring for a chat, please don't be upset. They don't mean any harm. They're soft-hearted, really. And in any case, solid Yi Mun-gu will be the neighborhood chief in charge of things).

But who can that white-haired madman be,
that fellow roaming Gwanghwamun crossroads, clothes undone, with
a face dark from drinking, hair like a bush, loose pants,
at this sorrowful time?

An Old Well

I write that I'm like an old spider,

a chipped bowl lying in the yard of an empty house,

a frost-covered riverbank path in early morning,

a crow on a midwinter's evening,

the cheap statue of Admiral Yi Sunshin at a closed-down school.

I'm like the old ashtray of a taxi driver on the ourskirts of a town,

an old well nobody visits,

a sponge long ago discarded beside it.

I write that I'm like Cheoyong shutting the door and weakly turning away.

Like the howl of a dog that's been winding round your calves.

I write that I'm like urine one passes after waking alone in the dead of night.

I absolutely do not write that I'm lonely.

Vale of Tears (Sabha)

With this, farewell to the year.

A remote roadside where weeds are one by one packing up their stands.
One aged ant is employing all its strength to drag along
a young green cricket (only a few days since its birth!)
flailing its slender legs.

On being asked to let the creature go, should it still be alive,
the ant stubbornly insists it's dead.

It won't let go.

Empty House

Standing before the gate, I call you.
In a trembling voice I call your name.
The sound is too loud for my ears alone.
No answer comes, of course.
I kick the closed gate.
When no answer comes I swear loudly,
calling you a bitch.

I only come freely when the house is empty.
I sit leaning against the cold gate and feel
the sound of your feet climbing the steps,
your fingers fumbling for the keys,
the scar on the back of the hand twisting the doorknob,
your body sucked in through the door, the briefly swelling flared skirt
with its chickweed pattern,
your soft calves.
Sounds seep out faintly through the crack of the door.

I lick up your lingering scent with a long tongue.
I caress the steps you trod.
My fingertips ache as though pressed down by your heels,
but I can endure it, this weight and the rounded hips.
My hand trembles, here before the empty house.

Bullet Fee

Kaveh Alipour, aged nineteen, was killed, shot in the head at an intersection in downtown Teheran while returning home (June 20, 2009).
Told he would have to pay a $3,000 "bullet fee" before his son's body could be handed over,
the impoverished father insisted, in tears, that his entire fortune didn't amount to such a sum so he'd have to abandon the body,
at which he was told that if the funeral was held outside the city
the bullet fee would be waived.
It seems the young man was still unmarried, one week to go until his wedding. (Inshallah!)

Hurrah, hurrah, bullets here and bullets there, bang, one for Father off to work, one for Mother weary from doing laundry, one for older sister milking sheep, bang, one for me, too, heck, I didn't want to go to school anyway, a bang for each while the prices are low, one bang for each and everyone.
Three thousand dollars is already dirt cheap, but if you do as you're told, it's free.
Goods released for clearance, heartbreak bankruptcy sale,
top trending on the web is "today's bullet price."

When bullets come flying, dodge them until checking today's market price.
When the price is right, rush out and receive them liberally.
Likewise with the water cannons:
shower facility fees, water fees, plus labor costs,
the clubs made of imported wood, and what about the service fees?
It's global common sense today that even protests require money,
and with not even enough for the bullet fee,
might as well just go home and eat pancakes.
What's the point of demonstrating?
To register for a demonstration, you have to put down a deposit for the bullet fees, the water fees, and miscellaneous labor charges,
and you have to fix a price for loudspeakers. The cost of unauthorized

abuse to the auditory nerves of unspecified masses, compensation for interrupting the work of nearby office workers, the expected psychological trauma resulting from that, and what else, a guarantee of insurance premiums for post-traumatic stress disorder, and insurance premiums to cover those premiums.

So that's the story with Iran
that people are exempt from bullet fees
if they carry the body far away.

Hour K

Hour K, aged forty-eight years and nine months, has been spilt.
It remains puddled on its side, snoring.
It is camouflaged as a solid.
Hour's swollen, dirty ankles
protrude from ragged pants.
Long exposed to soju, Hour K is flushed.
Sticky saliva has flowed, linking its face to the ground.
Hour K has itchy sides and itchy armpits.
Though it scratches, they do not break open.
There is no place suitable for it to flow to, even asleep.
Trapped in a dirty bag, the hour is rotting away. If the plastic bursts
it will flow away like feeble tears.
After briefly moistening a corner in the underpass
with a sour smell,
it'll soon dry. Non-regular hours
will come along pushing a mop.

Ghostlike hours, bags of hours.

No Shadows

The woman beside me pulls out a hand mirror and applies rouge. The short-skirted young woman opposite frees her fishnet-stockinged feet and rests them on her shoes, while beside her a guy in his fifties wearing high-waisted pants spreads his legs wide and stares up and down at the passers-by. The young girl hanging onto a strap, engrossed in a phone call, has already vanished, leaving only her navel and waist behind, and the white flesh glimpsed through the rips in the jeans of the yellow-haired student in front of her, shaking his feet as he taps out a text message look painful.

They're all descendants of families with home villages where the ancestors had graves, where older and younger branches of the family lived, with paths between paddy fields, streams at the foot of the facing hills, where there were cherry blossom days at the wellside, where Grandfather in his study would loudly clear his throat and spit with dignity.

When will we all meet again?
We wouldn't recognize one another even if we did. For we
have no shadows.

A Dream

"This year," I write,
and the two words turn into white popcorn bouncing off the page.
There are days when they puff up into the snowbell tree's white blossoms.
Whenever my wife sighs, always lacking money,
I fly to a corner of the room and feign ignorance,
turn into a middle-aged quince tree, gentle and fragrant for ages.
When the children return home tired,
the tree that I am goes plodding through winter rain
as far as Peace Market.
The instant the red light changes,
the quick-delivery motorbike brigades with their bated breath
turn into a flock of seagulls and all together fly into the sky.
Gracefully they swoop down over Udo Island, Jido Island,
on really good days venture as far as Daemado Island.
One homeless fellow, rubbing his swollen feet,
startled by the seagulls, rams against the wall of the underpass
and turns into a black-backed whale,
goes gliding calmly through the ocean depths,
round the Kuril Islands, as far as the Cape of Good Hope.

"This year, I pray," I write to mail,
until white popcorn comes bouncing up,
until seagulls and whales come back home.

Learning

It's all very good
once I say:
"It's all learning."
The burden of Mother's parting,
the burden of staying behind and seeing her off.
Once I say:
"Mother's embarked on her last bit of great learning,"
I'm a boy again kneeling at a low writing desk.

I feel as though a large, warm hand will come from somewhere,
stroke my head: You're working hard.
Lowering my eyes,
bashful,
I won't be able to say a word
but inwardly grateful, sorrowful,
my eyes will swim with tears.

Night falling
rain falling,
wind blowing,
dead leaves falling and new buds sprouting,
one going, another coming,
at times standing by their side, immersed in thought.

It's easier to endure if I say: "It's all learning."

Sutra of the Void

He was born the son of a poor farmer.
After dropping out of school
he wanted to become a boxer
but worked as a construction laborer instead.
Life grew harder once he was married
so he went back home and farmed the land.
After losing everything, he came back to Seoul,
back to construction sites,
then suffered kidney failure.
He'd closed the education savings account for his three children,
was two months past due for rice on credit, when
a notice arrived declaring their illegal home was to be demolished.
He went up into the hills and hanged himself.
There being no land to lay him in,
he was scattered in the void, again, a handful of ash,
aged forty-two.

Three Days after the Funeral

Two measures of black beans are frying in a pan.
After the black beans have been cooked and brought in,
eighty-year-old father, his younger son, and the granddaughter sit round,
eating the beans.

Mother has gone,
summer rains are coming,
but nobody worries about
the new grave mound;
they simply munch the beans.

Three generations sit around the bowl of beans
and stare blankly at the television,
the pounding, frolicking television.

Dedicated To Silence

You've crossed the river and fallen asleep;
weary, you gently snore
while I, I lean on the snowflakes
seeping into the river beyond the window,
and drift along, following a heartless Western song.
For fear that your deep sleep will waver,
I cautiously empty the final glass,
mindful even of the sound of my gurgling throat.
Having buried you in the sweet sleep across the river,
this lonesome peace we enjoy here,
thinking neither this nor that,
daybreak mist
rising deafeningly.

Notes on the Poems

"Someone Who Makes a Bridge Feel Lonely" - The inserted texts are from two poems by Yi Seong-seon (1941 – 2001).

"Memorial to the Filial Devotion of Lee from Gyeongju" - The stone from the mid-Joseon period with this inscription is located in Sinwang-ri, Hyeondeok-myeon, Pyeongtaek City, Gyeonggi Province.

"A Girl Hunched by the Fire Making Dough Flakes Soup—I Will Be Her Man" - The title is a line from Kim Myeong-in's poem, "A Shingle-Roofed House."

Pole Star - Polaris, a star in Ursa Minor, which when seen from the Northern Hemisphere, seems never to move in the sky and so serves to indicate due North.

Gyodong hill - Gyodong is a neighborhood in Jeonju, the main city of North Jeolla Province.

In a traditional Korean house, the *maru* is a wood-floored, roofed space opening onto the yard between individual rooms.

"Buried in the Sea at Yerae" - Yerae is a seaside village on Jeju Island. The island, of volcanic origin, lies south of South Jeolla Province and is a World Heritage Site.

"Gunha-ri in Winter" - Gunha-ri is a neighborhood in Gimpo City, west of Seoul.

"Nobody Knows" - Fivestones is a game similar to jacks.

Pasqueflower is a form of anemone.

"At Yeongweol" - Yeongweol is a county in Gangwon Province, east of Seoul.

"Friends" - Paduk is the Korean name for a board game widely known by its Japanese name, "Go."

"Depths of a Landscape 2" - Jochiwon is a township located in South Chungcheong Province.

"Rainy Season" - The Suta Temple of Mt Gongjak is a Buddhist shrine at the foot of the Gongjak Mountain. It is a national monument that was built in 708, in stone, by the Buddhist priest WonHyo during the reign of King SeongDeok, the 33rd King of Silla.

Mt. Gongjak is located in Hongcheon County, a county and city in Gangwon Province in northeastern South Korea.

"Busy, Busy" - Nightjars are medium-sized nocturnal birds with long wings, short legs and very short bills.

Celadines are yellow-flowered Eurasian biennial herbs (Chelidonium majus) of the poppy family.

"Hwajin" - Hwajin is a girl's name.

"Has Love Come?" - Simcheong appears in a famous Korean folktale and is a symbol of filial piety. Simcheong lost her mother at birth. Though her father tried his best to take care of her, he became blind. One day, a Buddhist monk told him he would recover his sight if he offered 300 sacks of rice to his temple. Learning this, his daughter sold herself to merchants to serve as a sacrifice for a safe sea journey in exchange for 300 sacks of rice. Leaping into the sea, she descended to the palace of the Dragon king. The great king admired her virtue and sent her back to land in a lotus flower. She gave a banquet for all blind men and was finally reunited with her father, whose eyes opened so he could see her.

"Thaw" - Mount Simhak is in Paju, just west of Seoul.

Jeon Bong-jun was a leader of the 1894 Donghak Peasant Uprising, where ordinary people rose up against the rampant corruption of the ruling classes

"Deokpyeong Market" - Deokpyeong is a township in Jiksan-eup, Seobuk-gu, Cheonan-si, South Chungcheong Province, where a traditional open-air market is held on every fifth day.

Acorn jelly is a Korean food made from acorn starch.

Dorco sets are sets of shaving implements.

"Cockscomb" - Na Hun-a was a popular "trot" singer who debuted in 1966.

"Off to New York" - *Haigo-ya* is an exclamation expressing intense pleasure.

"A Lucid Sound" - Deokwon temple is a Buddhist temple in Ulsan, South-eastern Korea.

"The Night Before Lunar New Year" - Suda-sa temple is in Gumi, North Gyeongsang Province

"YOL" - Yol is a celebrated Turkish film from 1982, written by Yılmaz Güney, about three prisoners who escape from prison but fail to find freedom.

"Injeolmi Rice Cakes" - Injeolmi is rice cake made with sweet rice (glutinous rice). It's one of the most popular and common Korean rice cakes.

Sujebi soup - A trditional Korean soup made with hand-pulled dough flakes roughly torn by hand, cooked with various vegetables

"Yellow Shirt" is the title of a popular song.

Yongsan Market is located in Seoul.

"Public Holiday" - Chungrang Bridge crosses a stream in eastern Seoul.

"Yeosu" - Suncheon is a coastal city in South Jeolla Province.

Sinweol-dong is a neighborhood of Yangcheon-gu in Yeosu, South Jeolla Province.

Gwangju is the capital city in South Jeolla Province in Southwestern Korea.

"Mokpo" - Mokpo is a port city in South Jeolla Province.

Ui-do - An island in Buan County, North Jeolla Province

"There Is No Fighting Against Such Odds" - The quoted line is borrowed from Maroyama Noboru's "Lu Xun."

"Bak Yeong-geun" - The poet Bak Yeong-geun lived in Buan, North Jeolla Province, died aged forty-eight on May 11, 2006.

"Foolish Desert" - *Foolish Desert* is the title of the fourth collection of poems by the poet Shin Hyeon-jeong, who died on October 16, 2009.

Kim Jong-sam (1921 - 1984) was a much admired Korean poet.

Cheon Sang-byeong (1930 - 1993) was a much loved poet who lived in great poverty.

Bak Yong-nae (1925 - 1980) was a poet who died while still relatively young.

Chae Gwang-seok (1948 - 1987) was a young poet killed in a traffic accident.

Bak Yeong-geun (1958 - 2006) was a working-class poet.

Yi Mun-gu (1941 - 2003) was a highly-esteemed novelist.

Gwanghwamun crossroads - The central intersection in front of Gyeongbok-gung Palace in the middle of Seoul.

"An Old Well" - Admiral Yi Sunshin (1545 – 1598) is Korea's greatest national hero. A naval commander famed for his victories against the Japanese navy during the Imjin war, when Japan invaded Korea in the 1590s. He died in battle.

Cheoyong - According to an account in *The Legends and History of the Three Kingdoms [Samguk Yusa]*, Cheoyong was a legendary figure of the Silla period who was rewarded with an official rank as well as a beautiful wife for his service to the kingdom. Upon returning home one day and finding his wife in bed with an evil-spirit-turned-man, Cheoyong woefully turned away and withdrew.

"Vale of Tears" - *Sabha* is the Buddhist term for this present world of pain and illusion, corresponding to the Christian expression "Vale of Tears."

"A Dream" - Peace Market is a large clothing market beside the East Gate in Seoul.

Udo Island is located 2.2 miles off the coast of Jeju Island.

Jido Island is a little to the North of Udo Island.

Daemado Island is the Korean name of a Japanese island situated in the Korea Strait, approximately halfway between the Japanese mainland and the Korean Peninsula. Its Japanese name is Tsushima.

The Kuril Islands lies in Russia's Sakhalin Oblast region. They stretch approximately 1,300 km (700 miles) northeast from Hokkaido, Japan, to Kamchatka, Russia, separating the Sea of Okhotsk from the North Pacific Ocean.

The Poet

Kim Sa-in was born in Boeun, North Chungcheon Province, in 1955. He has published three collections of poetry, *Night Letters* (*bame sseuneun pyeonji*, 1987), *Liking in Silence* (*gamanhi joahaneun*, 2006), and *Beside a Baby Donkey* (*eorin dangnagui gyeoteseo*, 2015), collections of criticism, including *A Deep Reading of the Novels of Park Sang-Ryung* (2001), and essays, *A Warm Bowl of Rice* (2006). Following time in prison in the early 1980s he began writing poetry and co-founded the magazine *Poetry and Economy.* In late 2010 he participated in the University of Iowa's International Writing Program. Among his awards are the Sin Dong-Yeop Grant for Writing (1987), the Modern Literature Prize for poetry (2005), and the Daesan Literature Award for poetry (2006). He taught creative writing at Dongdeok Women's University, and hosted broadcast programs devoted to poetry and spirituality. Since early 2018 he is the Director of the Literature Translation Institute of Korea.

The Translators

Brother Anthony was born in 1942 in England and completed his studies in the University of Oxford before becoming a member of the Community of Taizé (France) in 1969. Since 1980, he has been living in Korea and teaching English literature at Sogang University, where he is now an Emeritus Professor. He is a Chair Professor in Dankook University. He has published some forty volumes of English translations of modern Korean literature, mostly poetry, including works by Jeong Ho-Seung, Oh Sae-Young, Do Jong-Hwan, Ku Sang, Ko Un, Yi Si-Young, Kim Soo-Bok, and Yi Mun-yol. He is also the author of *The Korean Way of Tea* and of *Korean Tea Classics.* He took Korean citizenship in 1994 and An Sonjae is his official Korean name. He received the Korean government's Award of Merit, Jade Crown class, in October 2008 for his work in promoting knowledge of Korean literature in the world. In 2015 he was awarded an MBE by Queen Elizabeth for his contributions to Korean-British relations.

Home page: http://anthony.sogang.ac.kr/

Susan Hwang is assistant professor of contemporary Korean literature and cultural studies at Indiana University Bloomington. She is currently completing a manuscript for a book on the protest culture of the 1970s and '80s in South Korea.

Korean Voices Series

Liking in Silence
Poems by Kim Sa-in
Translated by Brother Anthony of Taizé & Susan Hwang
VOLUME 27 978-1-945680-34-2. $17.00

What Makes a City?
Stories by Park Seongwon
Translated by Chung Hwa Chang & Andrew Keast
VOLUME 26 978-1-945680-20-5 186 PAGES. $16.00

We, Day by Day
Poetry by Jin Eun-young
Translated by Daniel Parker & YoungShil Ji
VOLUME 25 978-1-945680-11-3 88 PAGES. $16.00

Nobody Checks the Time When They're Happy
Stories by Eun Heekyung
Translated by Amber Kim
VOLUME 24 978-1-945680-08-3 178 PAGES. $16.00

Wolves
A Novel by Jeon Sungtae
Translated by Sora Kim Russell
VOLUME 23 978-1-945680-01-4 192 PAGES $16.00

Someone Always in the Corner of My Eye
Poems by BoSeon Shim
Translated by Daniel Parker & YoungShil Ji
VOLUME 22 978-1-935210-90-0 94 PAGES $16.00

Wild Apple
Poems by HeeDuk Ra
Translated by Daniel Parker & YoungShil Ji
VOLUME 21 978-1-934210-73-3 90 PAGES $17.99

Modern Family
A Novel by Cheon Myeong-Kwan
Translated by Kyoung-lee Park
VOLUME 20 978-1-934210-67-2 180 PAGES $16.00

I Must Be the Wind
Poems by Moon Chung-hee
Translated by Clare You & Richard Silberg
VOLUME 19 978-1-935210-60-3 118 PAGES $16.00

One Day, Then Another
Poems by Kim Kwang-Kyu
Translated by Cho Young-Shil
VOLUME 18 978-1-935210-54-2 104 PAGES $16.00

Magnolia & Lotus: Selected Poems of Hyesim
Translated by Ian Haight & T'ae-yong Ho
VOLUME 17 978-1-935210-43-6 96 PAGES $16.00

This Side of Time: Selected Poems by Ko Un
Translated by Claire You & Richard Silberg
VOLUME 16 978-1-935210-32-0 100 PAGES $16.00

Borderland Roads: Selected Poems of Ho Kyun
Translated by Ian Haight & T'ae-yong Ho
VOLUME 15 978-1-935210-08-5 102 PAGES $16.00

Scale and Stairs: Selected Poems of Heeduk Ra
Translated by Won-chung Kim & Christopher Merrill
VOLUME 14 978-1-893996-24-3 88 PAGES $17.00

One Human Family & Other Stories
Stories by Chung Yeun-hee
Translated by Hyun-jae Yee Sallee
VOLUME 13 978-1-893996-87-8 232 PAGES $16.00

Woman on the Terrace
Poems by Moon Chung-hee
Translated by Seong-kon Kim & Alec Gordon
VOLUME 12 978-1-873996-86-1 120 PAGES $18.00

Eyes of Dew
Poems by Chonggi Mah
Translated by Brother Anthony of Taizé
VOLUME 11 1-893996-79-4 160 PAGES $16.00

Even Birds Leave the World: Selected Poems of Ji-woo Hwang
Translated by Won-chun Kim & Christopher Merrill
VOLUME 10 1-893996-45-X 104 PAGES $14.00

The Depths of a Clam: Selected Poems of Kim Kwang-kyu
Translated by Brother Anthony of Taize
VOLUME 9 1-893996-43-3 160 PAGES $16.00

Echoing Song: Contemporary Korean Women Poets
Edited by Peter H. Lee
VOLUME 8 1-893996-35-2 304 PAGES $18.00

Among the Flowering Reeds: Classic Korean Poems in Chinese
Edited and translated by Kim Jong-gil
VOLUME 7 1-893996-54-9 152 PAGES $16.00

Brother Enemy: Poems of the Korean War
Edited and translated by Suh Ji-moon
VOLUME 6 1-893996-20-4 176 PAGES $16.00

Shrapnel and Other Stories
Stories of Dong-ha Lee
Translated by Hyun-jae Yee Sallee
VOLUME 5 1-893996-53-0 176 PAGES $16.00

Strong Wind At Mishi Pass
Poems by Tong-gyu Hwang
Translated by Seong-kon Kim & Dennis Maloney
VOLUME 4 1-893996-10-7 118 PAGES $15.00

A Sketch of the Fading Sun
Stories of Wan-suh Park
Translated by Hyun-jae Yee Sallee
VOLUME 3 1-877727-93-8 200 PAGES $15.00

Heart's Agony: Selected Poems of Chiha Kim
Translated by Won-chun Kim & James Han
VOLUME 2 1-877727-84-9 128 PAGES $14.00

The Snowy Road: An Anthology of Korean Fiction
Translated by Hyun-jae Yee Sallee
VOLUME 1 1-877727-19-9 168 PAGES $12.00